MY FIRST
ENGLISH-SPANISH
PICTURE DICTIONARY

Publications International, Ltd.

Illustrations: Ted Williams; Karol Kaminski.

Contributing writer:
Lyn McLean has taught Spanish at all levels, trained teachers, authored Spanish textbooks, and produced videos and Web sites. She lived in Mexico for ten years and has traveled widely in the Spanish-speaking world. She is the founder and director of Children's Language Institute.

Louis Weber, CEO
Publications International, Ltd.
7373 North Cicero Avenue
Lincolnwood, Illinois 60712

Permission is never granted for commercial purposes.

Manufactured in China.

8 7 6 5 4 3 2 1

ISBN-13: 978-1-4127-1086-2
ISBN-10: 1-4127-1086-3

Contents

Índice de Materias
(in-dee-say day mah-**tayr**-ee-ahs)

Introduction

Introduccíon (een-tro-dook-see-**ohn**)

A note to parents

My First English-Spanish Picture Dictionary is a colorful and exciting way to learn Spanish. This book is designed to make learning Spanish fun and to appeal to a variety of learning styles.

- Looking at illustrations helps visual learners see the connection between the Spanish words and the real world.

- Seeing the word in English and then in Spanish helps those who learn better by seeing a word-to-word translation.

- Hearing the words pronounced in Spanish as they see the words and pictures helps those who learn better by listening.

A picture dictionary is an excellent format for introducing children to a new language. *My First English-Spanish Picture Dictionary* features more than 600 illustrations of objects that are familiar to children. Each illustration is accompanied by both the English and Spanish word as well as a phonetic pronunciation guide. Words and illustrations are grouped by themes, which makes them easy to find and easier to remember.

The pronunciation guides

A unique feature of *My First English-Spanish Picture Dictionary* is the phonetic pronunciation guide accompanying each Spanish word. Using this guide, even non-Spanish speakers can say the word out loud. After you have repeated the word several times, encourage children to say the word with you, and then alone if they wish. If they are not ready at first to say the word with you, don't worry. Many children prefer to listen first and absorb the sounds of the language before they speak.

Don't be shy about pronouncing the Spanish words to your children. The more you model the speech, the quicker your children will pick it up. As you and your children learn together, be as enthusiastic and encouraging as possible. Learning a new language can be a little intimidating, but this approach will help build your children's confidence in both understanding and speaking Spanish.

Using the book

You can use *My First English-Spanish Picture Dictionary* in many ways depending on the age and interests of your children. The illustrated table of contents gives you a colorful overview of the themes. Visit the themes in any order you wish. After you look at the illustrations and repeat the words, you can play a variety of language games. Say a word, and ask your children to point to the word you have just said or the picture that matches it. Later, point to a picture and ask for the word in Spanish. Time yourselves, and see who can say the word or find the picture the fastest. You can play charades or a modified version of the Pictionary board game in Spanish as well. *My First English-Spanish Picture Dictionary* provides endless possibilities for learning new Spanish words in entertaining ways.

As you read this book, use it as an opportunity to teach basic reading and organization skills. Pick a theme, and ask your children to find it in the table of contents and then turn to the correct page. You can also use the Spanish or English index to teach children how to locate information in a book.

Some tips about Spanish
Most Spanish nouns are preceded by **la** or **el,** which mean "the." When learning Spanish, it is a good idea to memorize the **la** or **el** with each word. This is because all Spanish nouns, such as *boy* (el muchacho) and *girl* (la muchacha), as well as *book* (el libro) and *doll* (la muñeca), are masculine or feminine. **La** is feminine, and **el** is masculine. If a word is

plural, **los** or **las** comes before it; for example, *boys* (los muchachos) and *girls* (las muchachas). **Los** is masculine, and **las** is feminine.

The pronunciation guide beneath each word explains the pronunciation of the word and indicates which part of each word is stressed. If a word has more than one syllable, the stressed syllable is indicated in **bold.**

Some Spanish words are written with an **ñ**, which is the letter **n** with a tilde over it. In Spanish the ñ is a separate letter of the alphabet and is pronounced more like **ny** in English. For example *el baño* (the bathroom) is pronounced /el **bah**-nyo/.

Some words have accents. An accent doesn't change the sound of a letter, but it changes the way the word is spoken. For example, in *la mamá* (mommy) the accent over the **a** means that the last syllable is stressed (said the loudest): /lah mah-**mah**/.

Even if your accent is not perfect, if you say the words as they are written, a Spanish-speaking person will understand you and will probably be delighted that you are learning Spanish!

mother
la madre
(lah **mah**-dray)

father
el padre
(el **pah**-dray)

grandfather
el abuelo
(el ah-**bway**-lo)

grandmother
la abuela
(lah ah-**bway**-lah)

uncle
el tío
(el **tee**-o)

aunt
la tía
(lah **tee**-ah)

baby
el bebé
(el bay-**bay**)

brother
el hermano
(el ayr-**mah**-no)

sister
la hermana
(lah ayr-**mah**-nah)

cousin
la prima/el primo
(lah **pree**-mah/el **pree**-mo)

to hug
abrazar
(ah-brah-**sahr**)

to kiss
besar
(bay-**sahr**)

to laugh
reír
(ray-**eer**)

to love
amar
(ah-**mahr**)

to tickle
dar cosquillas
(dahr kos-**kee**-yahs)

Let's Talk
¡Hablamos!
(ah-**blah**-mos)

Do you have any brothers or sisters?
¿Tienes hermanos?
(tee-**en**-ays ayr-**mah**-nos)

Yes. I have one brother.
Sí. Tengo un hermano.
(see **tayn**-go oon ayr-**mah**-no)

Face

La **cara** (lah **cah**-rah)

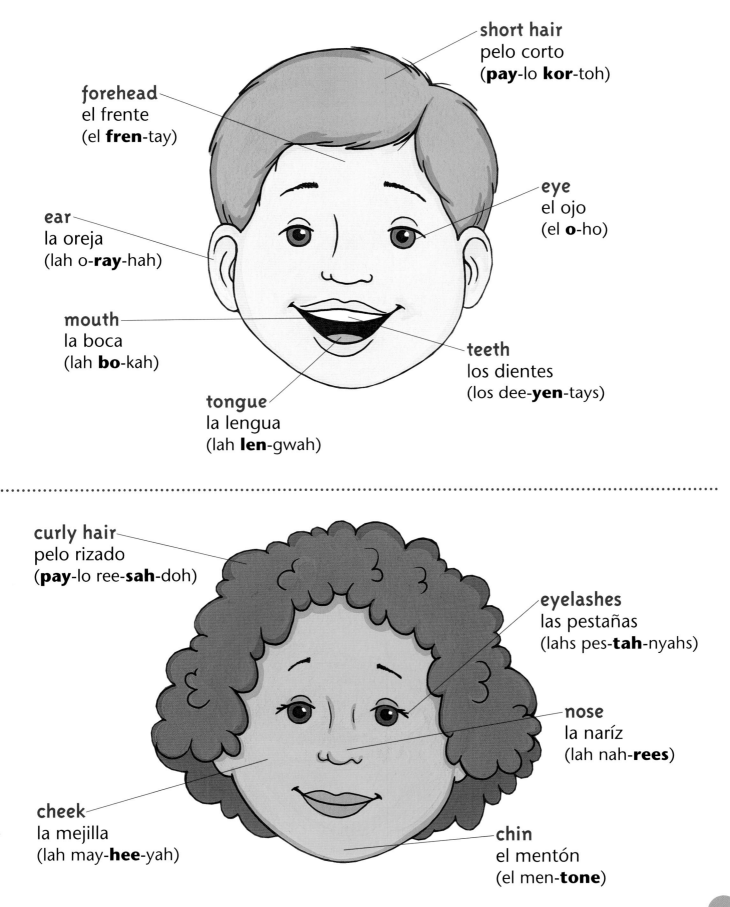

short hair
pelo corto
(**pay**-lo **kor**-toh)

forehead
el frente
(el **fren**-tay)

eye
el ojo
(el **o**-ho)

ear
la oreja
(lah o-**ray**-hah)

mouth
la boca
(lah **bo**-kah)

teeth
los dientes
(los dee-**yen**-tays)

tongue
la lengua
(lah **len**-gwah)

curly hair
pelo rizado
(**pay**-lo ree-**sah**-doh)

eyelashes
las pestañas
(lahs pes-**tah**-nyahs)

nose
la naríz
(lah nah-**rees**)

cheek
la mejilla
(lah may-**hee**-yah)

chin
el mentón
(el men-**tone**)

glasses
los lentes
(los **len**-tays)

straight hair
pelo lacio
(**pay**-lo **lah**-see-o)

bald
calvo
(**kahl**-vo)

eyebrows
las cejas
(lahs **say**-hahs)

long hair
pelo largo
(**pay**-lo **lahr**-go)

beard
la barba
(lah **bar**-bah)

Let's Talk

¡Hablamos!
(ah-**blah**-mos)

What beautiful eyes you have!
¡Qué ojos tan bonitos tienes!
(kay **o**-hos tahn bo-**nee**-tohs tee-**en**-ays)

Thank you.
Gracias.
(**grah**-see-ahs)

El **cuerpo** (el kwayr-po)

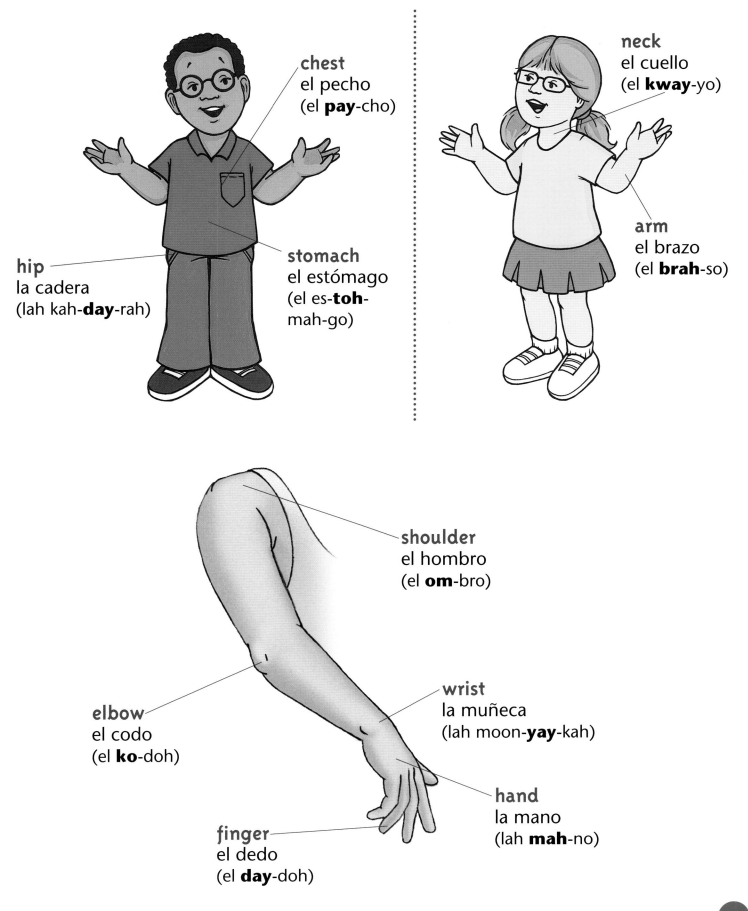

chest
el pecho
(el **pay**-cho)

hip
la cadera
(lah kah-**day**-rah)

stomach
el estómago
(el es-**toh**-
mah-go)

neck
el cuello
(el **kway**-yo)

arm
el brazo
(el **brah**-so)

shoulder
el hombro
(el **om**-bro)

elbow
el codo
(el **ko**-doh)

wrist
la muñeca
(lah moon-**yay**-kah)

hand
la mano
(lah **mah**-no)

finger
el dedo
(el **day**-doh)

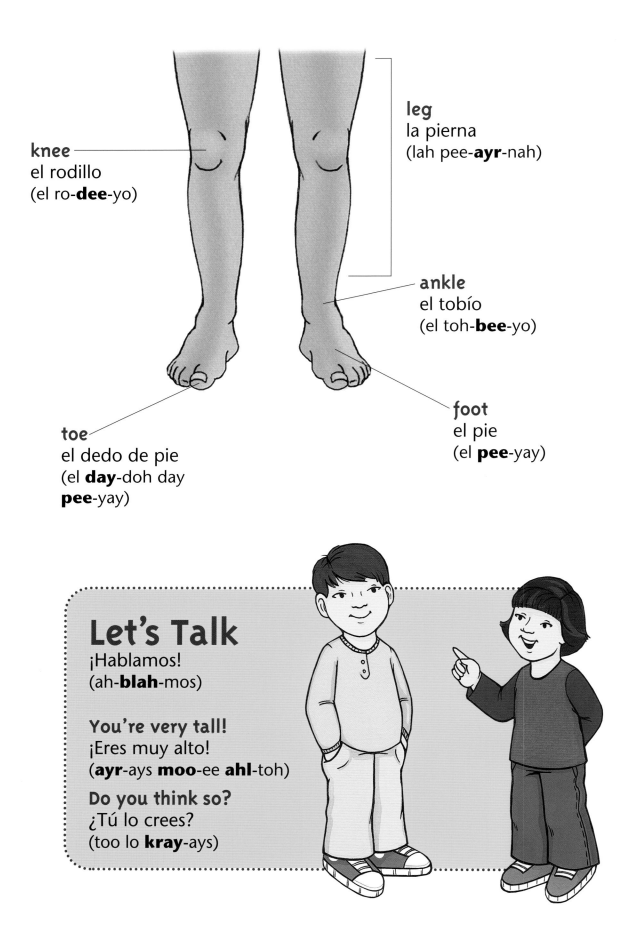

knee
el rodillo
(el ro-**dee**-yo)

leg
la pierna
(lah pee-**ayr**-nah)

ankle
el tobío
(el toh-**bee**-yo)

toe
el dedo de pie
(el **day**-doh day
pee-yay)

foot
el pie
(el **pee**-yay)

Let's Talk
¡Hablamos!
(ah-**blah**-mos)

You're very tall!
¡Eres muy alto!
(**ayr**-ays **moo**-ee **ahl**-toh)

Do you think so?
¿Tú lo crees?
(too lo **kray**-ays)

T-shirt
la camiseta
(lah kah-mee-**say**-tah)

blouse
la blusa
(lah **bloo**-sah)

jeans
los vaqueros
(los vah-**kay**-ros)

shirt
la camisa
(lah kah-**mee**-sah)

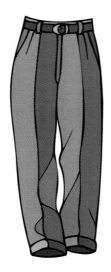

pants
los pantalones
(los pahn-tah-**lo**-nays)

shorts
los pantalones cortos
(los pahn-tah-**lo**-nays
cor-tohs)

sweater
el suéter
(el **swe**-tayr)

underpants
los pantalones interiores
(los pahn-tah-**lo**-nays
in-tayr-ee-**or**-ays)

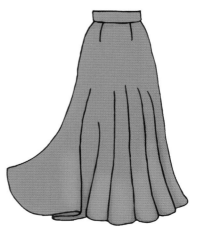

skirt
la falda
(lah **fahl**-dah)

dress
el vestido
(el ves-**tee**-doh)

jacket
la chaqueta
(lah chah-**kay**-tah)

bathrobe
la bata
(lah **bah**-tah)

socks
los calcetines
(los kahl-say-**tee**-nays)

raincoat
el impermeable
(el im-per-mee-**ah**-blay)

pajamas
el pijama
(el pee-**hah**-mah)

scarf
la bufanda
(lah boo-**fahn**-dah)

mittens
los mitones
(los mee-**toh**-nays)

gloves
los guantes
(los **gwahn**-tays)

shoes
los zapatos
(los sah-**pah**-tohs)

boots
las botas
(lahs **bo**-tahs)

to put on
ponerse
(po-**nayr**-say)

sneakers
los zapatos de lona
(los sah-**pah**-tohs day
lo-nah)

hat
el gorro
(el **go**-ro)

to take off
quitarse
(kee-**tahr**-say)

Let's Talk
¡Hablamos!
(ah-**blah**-mos)

I like your sweater.
Me gusta tu suéter.
(may **goo**-stah too **swe**-tayr)

Thank you. It's new.
Gracias. Es nuevo.
(**grah**-see-ahs ays noo-**ay**-vo)

watch
el reloj
(el ray-**lo**)

bracelet
la pulsera
(lah pool-**say**-rah)

barrette
broche para el cabello
(**bro**-chay **pah**-rah el kah-**bay**-yo)

gold
oro
(**o**-ro)

necklace
el collar
(el koy-**yahr**)

ring
el anillo
(el ah-**nee**-yo)

silver
plata
(**plah**-tah)

earrings
los aretes
(los ah-**ray**-tays)

Let's Talk
¡Hablamos!
(ah-**blah**-mos)

What time is it?
¿Qué hora es?
(kay **o**-rah ays)

It's three o'clock.
Son las tres.
(sown lahs trays)

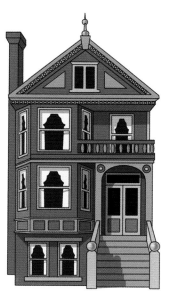

house
la casa
(lah **kah**-sah)

roof
el techo
(el **tay**-cho)

attic
el desvan
(el des-**vahn**)

bedroom
el dormitorio
(el dor-mee-**tor**-ee-o)

bathroom
el baño
(el **bah**-nyo)

living room
la sala
(lah **sah**-lah)

dining room
el comedor
(el ko-may-**dor**)

kitchen
la cocina
(lah ko-**see**-nah)

yard
el patio
(el **pah**-tee-o)

welcome mat
el tapete de bienvenido
(el tah-**pay**-tay day bee-yen-vay-**nee**-doh)

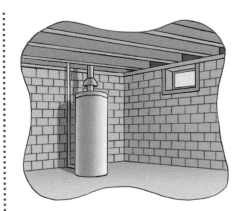

basement
el sótano
(el **so**-tah-no)

chimney
la chimenea
(lah chee-may-**nay**-ah)

stairs
las escaleras
(lahs es-kah-**lay**-rahs)

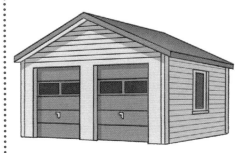

garage
el garaje
(el gah-**rah**-hay)

window
la ventana
(lah ven-**tah**-nah)

door
la puerta
(lah **pwayr**-tah)

Let's Talk
¡Hablamos!
(ah-**blah**-mos)

Do you live in a house or an apartment?
¿Vives en una casa o un apartamento?
(**vee**-vays en **oo**-nah **kah**-sah oh oon ah-pahr-tah-**men**-toh)

I live in a house.
Vivo en una casa.
(**vee**-vo en **oo**-nah **kah**-sah)

fireplace
el hogar
(el o-**gahr**)

couch
el sofá
(el so-**fah**)

curtain
la cortina
(lah kor-**tee**-nah)

chair
la silla
(lah **see**-yah)

rug
el tapete
(el tah-**pay**-tay)

telephone
el teléfono
(el tay-**lay**-fo-no)

Let's Talk
¡Hablamos!
(ah-**blah**-mos)

Let's watch TV.
Vamos a ver la televisión.
(**vah**-mos ah vayr lah
tay-lay-vee-see-**own**)

I want to read.
Yo quiero leer.
(yo kee-**ay**-oh lay-**ayr**)

lamp
la lámpara
(lah **lahm**-pah-rah)

El **dormitorio**
(el dor-mee-**tor**-ee-o)

bed
la cama
(lah **kah**-mah)

dresser
el tocador
(el toh-kah-**dor**)

blanket
la cobija
(lah ko-**bee**-hah)

pillow
la almohada
(lah ahl-mo-**ah**-dah)

alarm clock
el despertador
(el des-payr-tah-**dor**)

to sleep
dormir
(dor-**meer**)

Let's Talk
¡Hablamos!
(ah-**blah**-mos)

It's time to go to bed.
Es la hora de dormirse.
(ays lah **o**-rah day dor-**meer**-say)

¡One more story, please!
Un cuento más, por favor!
(oon **kwen**-toh mahs por fah-**vor**)

to dream
soñar
(so-**nyahr**)

Bathroom

El baño (el bah-nyo)

sink
el lavabo
(el lah-**vah**-bo)

soap
el jabón
(el hah-**bone**)

towel
la toalla
(lah toh-**eye**-yah)

toothbrush
el cepillo de dientes
(el say-**pee**-yo day
dee-**yen**-tays)

shampoo
el champú
(el shahm-**poo**)

toilet
el inodoro
(el ee-no-**doh**-ro)

Toothpaste

toothpaste
la pasta de dientes
(lah **pah**-stah day
dee-**yen**-tays)

bathtub
la tina
(lah **tee**-nah)

Let's Talk

¡Hablamos!
(ah-**blah**-mos)

I don't want to take a bath!
¡No quiero bañarme!
(no kee-**ay**-ro bah-**nyahr**-may)

You have to take a bath, honey.
Tienes que bañarte, mi cariño.
(tee-**en**-ays kay bah-**nyahr**-tay mee
kah-**ree**-nyo)

21

La **cocina** (lah ko-**see**-nah)

sink
el lavabo
(el lah-**vah**-bo)

pot
la olla
(lah oy-**yah**)

dishwasher
el lavaplatos
(el lah-vah-**plah**-tohs)

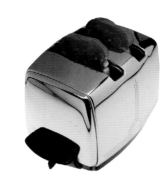

toaster
el tostador
(el toh-stah-**dor**)

stove
la estufa
(lah ays-**too**-fah)

refrigerator
el refrigerador
(el ray-free-gay-rah-**dor**)

frying pan
el sartén
(el sahr-**ten**)

Let's Talk

¡Hablamos!
(ah-**blah**-mos)

How many eggs do you want?
¿Cuántos huevos quieres?
(**kwahn**-tohs **way**-vos kee-**ay**-rays)

I want two, please.
Quiero dos, por favor.
(kee-**ay**-ro dohs por fah-**vor**)

bread
el pan
(el pahn)

milk
la leche
(lah **lay**-chay)

juice
el jugo
(el **hoo**-go)

cereal
el cereal
(el see-ray-**ahl**)

lemon
el limón
(el lee-**mone**)

egg
el huevo
(el **way**-vo)

orange
la naranja
(lah nah-**rahn**-hah)

cheese
el queso
(el **kay**-so)

chicken
el pollo
(el **po**-yo)

butter
la mantequilla
(lah mahn-tay-**kee**-yah)

steak
el bistéc
(el bee-**stek**)

ham
el jamón
(el hah-**mone**)

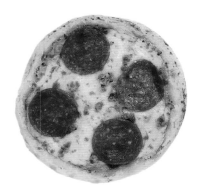

pizza
la pizza
(lah **peet**-sah)

fish
el pescado
(el pays-**kah**-doh)

lettuce
la lechuga
(lah lay-**choo**-gah)

cherries
las cerezas
(lahs say-**ray**-sahs)

peas
los guisantes
(los gee-**sahn**-tays)

carrots
las zanahorias
(lahs sah-nah-**oh**-ree-ahs)

corn
el maíz
(el **my**-ees)

banana
el plátano
(el **plah**-tah-no)

watermelon
la sandía
(lah sahn-**dee**-ah)

grapes
las uvas
(lahs **oo**-vahs)

strawberry
la fresa
(lah **fray**-sah)

apple
la manzana
(lah mahn-**sah**-nah)

tomato
el tomate
(el toh-**mah**-tay)

potatoes
las papas
(lahs **pah**-pahs)

Let's Talk

¡Hablamos!
(ah-**blah**-mos)

Do you like cheese?
¿Te gusta el queso?
(tay **goo**-stah el **kay**-so)

Yes, I love it!
¡Sí, me gusta mucho!
(see may **goo**-stah **moo**-cho)

breakfast
el desayuno
(el des-eye-**oo**-no)

spoon
la cuchara
(lah koo-**chah**-rah)

knife
el cuchillo
(el koo-**chee**-yo)

fork
el tenedor
(el ten-ay-**dor**)

lunch
el almuerzo
(el ahl-**mwayr**-so)

glass
el vaso
(el **vah**-so)

plate
el plato
(el **plah**-toh)

supper
la cena
(lah **say**-nah)

Let's Talk
¡Hablamos!
(ah-**blah**-mos)

I'm really hungry.
Tengo mucho hambre.
(**tayn**-go **moo**-cho **ahm**-bray)

So am I.
Yo también.
(yo tahm-bee-**en**)

washer
la lavadora
(lah lah-vah-**doh**-rah)

mop
el trapero
(el trah-**pay**-ro)

iron
la plancha
(lah **plahn**-chah)

dryer
la secadora
(lah say-kah-**doh**-rah)

dustpan
el recogedor
(el ray-ko-hay-**dor**)

ironing board
la tabla de planchar
(lah **tah**-bla day
plahn-**chahr**)

broom
la escoba
(lah ays-**ko**-bah)

Let's Talk
¡Hablamos!
(ah-**blah**-mos)

Where's the phone?
¿Dónde está el teléfono?
(**don**-day eh-**stah** el tay-**lay**-fo-no)

Here it is.
Aquí está.
(ah-**key** eh-**stah**)

Los **mascotas** (los mahs-**ko**-tahs)

dog
el perro
(el **pay**-ro)

puppies
los cachorros
(los kah-**cho**-ros)

mouse
el ratón
(el rah-**tone**)

turtle
la tortuga
(lah tor-**too**-gah)

cat
el gato
(el **gah**-toh)

kittens
los gatitos
(los gah-**tee**-tohs)

Let's Talk

¡Hablamos!
(ah-**blah**-mos)

Do you have a pet?
¿Tienes mascota?
(tee-**en**-ays mahs-**ko**-tah)

I have a dog, two cats, three rabbits, and a lot of fish.
Tengo un perro, dos gatos, tres conejos, y muchos peces.
(**tayn**-go oon **pay**-ro dos **gah**-tohs trays ko-**nay**-hos ee **moo**-chos **pay**-says)

guinea pig
el cobayo
(el ko-**bay**-yo)

flowerpot
la maceta
(lah mah-**say**-tah)

rose
la rosa
(lah **ro**-sah)

ladybug
la mariquita
(lah mah-ree-**kee**-tah)

soil
la tierra
(lah tee-**yay**-rah)

tulip
el tulipan
(el too-lee-**pahn**)

bee
la abeja
(lah ah-bay-**hah**)

seeds
las semillas
(lahs say-**mee**-yahs)

weed
la mala hierba
(lah **mah**-lah
ee-**ayr**-bah)

Let's Talk
¡Hablamos!
(ah-**blah**-mos)

What a beautiful day!
¡Qué día tan bonito!
(kay **dee**-yah tan bo-**nee**-toh)

And it's not too hot.
Y no hace demasiado calor.
(ee no **ah**-say day-mah-see-**ah**-doh kah-**lor**)

hammer
el martillo
(el mahr-**tee**-yo)

screwdriver
el destornillador
(el des-tor-nee-yah-**dor**)

screws
los tornillos
(los tor-**nee**-yos)

saw
el serrucho
(el say-**roo**-cho)

pliers
los alicates
(los ah-lee-**kah**-tays)

nails
los clavos
(los **klah**-vos)

Let's Talk

¡Hablamos!
(ah-**blah**-mos)

Do you want to help me?
¿Quieres ayudarme?
(kee-**ay**-rays ah-yoo-**dahr**-may)

Yes, Dad.
Sí, Papá.
(see pah-**pah**)

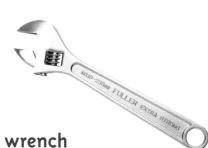

wrench
la llave fija
(lah **yah**-vay **fee**-hah)

stuffed animal
el animal de peluche
(el ah-nee-**mahl** day
pay-**loo**-chay)

dollhouse
la casa de muñecas
(lah **kah**-sah day
moo-**nyay**-kahs)

ball
la pelota
(lah pay-**lo**-tah)

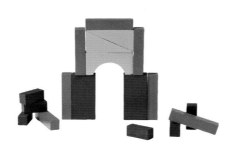

blocks
los bloques
(los **blo**-kays)

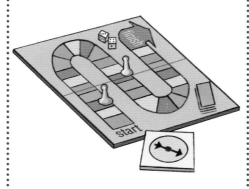

board game
el tablero
(el tah-**blay**-ro)

dice
los dados
(los **dah**-dohs)

toy cars
los carritos
(los kahr-**ree**-tohs)

soldiers
los soldaditos
(los sol-dah-**dee**-tohs)

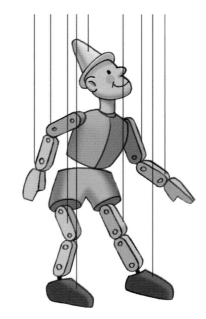

puppet
el títere
(el **tee**-tay-ray)

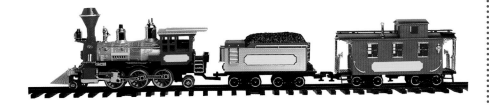

train
el tren
(el tren)

whistle
el silbato
(el seel-bah-**toh**)

video game
el juego de vídeo
(el **hway**-go day
vid-ay-o)

puzzle
el rompecabezas
(el rom-pay-kah-**bay**-sahs)

model airplane
la avioneta
(lah ah-vee-o-**nay**-tah)

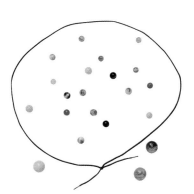

marbles
las canicas
(lahs kah-**nee**-kahs)

Let's Talk

¡Hablamos!
(ah-**blah**-mos)

What's your bear's name?
¿Cómo se llama tu oso?
(**ko**-mo say yah-**mah** too **o**-so)

Her name is Bear!
¡Se llama Oso!
(say **yah**-mah **o**-so)

Happy birthday!

¡Feliz cumpleaños! (fay-**lees** koom-plee-**ah**-nyos)

birthday cake
el pastel
(el pah-**stel**)

party hats
los gorros de fiesta
(los **go**-ros day fee-**es**-tah)

favors
los recuerdos
(los ray-**kwayr**-dohs)

present
el regalo
(el ray-**gah**-lo)

to sing
cantar
(kahn-**tahr**)

to blow out
soplar
(so-**plahr**)

balloons
los globos
(los **glo**-bos)

Let's Talk

¡Hablamos!
(ah-**blah**-mos)

Thank you for the present.
Gracias por el regalo.
(**grah**-see-ahs por el ray-**gah**-lo)

You're welcome. I hope you like it.
De nada. Espero que te guste.
(day **nah**-dah es-**pay**-ro kay tay **goo**-stay)

teacher
el maestro
(el mah-**yey**-stroh)

students
los alumnos
(los ah-**loom**-nos)

desk
el escritorio
(el es-kree-**tor**-ee-o)

chair
la silla
(lah **see**-yah)

blackboard
la pizarra
(lah pee-**sah**-rah)

to learn
aprender
(ah-pren-**dayr**)

ABC chart
el abecedario
(el ah-bay-say-**dah**-ree-o)

pencil
el lápiz
(el **lah**-pees)

eraser
el borrador
(el bo-rah-**dor**)

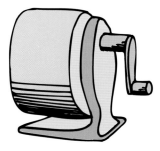

pencil sharpener
el sacapuntas
(el sah-kah-**poon**-tahs)

notebook
el cuaderno
(el kwah-**dayr**-no)

scissors
las tijeras
(lahs tee-**hay**-rahs)

paper
el papel
(el pah-**payl**)

book
el libro
(el **lee**-bro)

to pay attention
prestar atención
(prey-**stahr** ah-ten-see-**own**)

ruler
la regla
(lah **ray**-glah)

glue
el pegamento
(el pay-gah-**men**-toh)

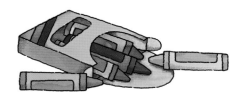

crayons
los crayones
(los kray-**o**-nays)

markers
los marcadores
(los mahr-kah-**doh**-rays)

paintbrushes
los pinceles
(los peen-**say**-lays)

to read
leer
(lay-**ayr**)

paint
la pintura
(lah peen-**too**-rah)

homework
la tarea
(lah tah-**ray**-ah)

to write
escribir
(es-kree-**beer**)

Let's Talk

¡Hablamos!
(ah-**blah**-mos)

What grade are you in?
¿En qué grado estás?
(en kay **grah**-doh es-**tahs**)

I'm in third grade.
Estoy en el tercero grado.
(eh-**stoy** en el ter-**say**-ro
grah-doh)

What a good job you did!
¡Qué buen trabajo hiciste!
(kay bwayn trah-**bah**-ho ee-
sees-tay)

Thank you, teacher.
Gracias, maestra.
(**grah**-see-ahs mah-**yey**-strah)

Musical instruments

Los **instrumentos musicales**
(los in-stroo-**mayn**-tohs moo-see-**kah**-lays)

guitar
la guitarra
(lah gee-**tah**-rah)

drum
el tambor
(el tahm-**bor**)

harmonica
la harmónica
(lah ahr-**mo**-nee-kah)

maracas
las maracas
(lahs mah-**rah**-kahs)

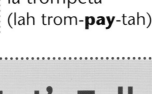

trumpet
la trompeta
(lah trom-**pay**-tah)

flute
la flauta
(lah **flau**-tah)

violin
el violín
(el vee-o-**leen**)

Let's Talk
¡Hablamos!
(ah-**blah**-mos)

Do you know how to play a musical instrument?
¿Sabes tocar un instrumento musical?
(**sah**-bays toh-**kahr** oon in-stroo-**mayn**-toh moo-see-**kahl**)

No, but I want to learn to play the piano.
No, pero quiero aprender a tocar el piano.
(no **pay**-ro kee-**ay**-ro ah-pren-**dayr** ah toh-**kahr** el pee-**ahn**-no)

monitor
la pantalla
(lah pahn-**ty**-yah)

to type
teclear
(tay-klay-**ahr**)

keyboard
la teclada
(lah tay-**klah**-dah)

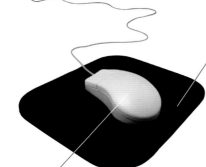

mouse pad
la alfombrilla para ratón
(lah ahl-fom-**bree**-yah
pah-rah rah-**tone**)

mouse
el ratón
(el rah-**tone**)

to turn on
encender
(en-sen-**dayr**)

laptop
la computadora portátil
(lah kom-poo-tah-**doh**-rah
por-**tah**-teel)

Let's Talk
¡Hablamos!
(ah-**blah**-mos)

I have a new computer game.
Tengo un juego de computadora nueva.
(**tayn**-go oon **hway**-go day kom-poo-tah-
doh-**rah** noo-**ay**-vah)

You're really lucky!
¡Qué suerte tienes!
(kay soo-**wer**-tay tee-**en**-ays)

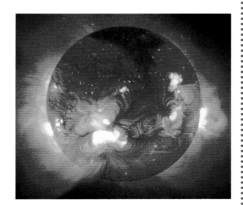

sun
el sol
(el sohl)

planet
la planeta
(lah plah-**nay**-tah)

telescope
el telescopio
(el tel-ay-**sko**-pee-o)

moon
la luna
(lah **loo**-nah)

earth
la tierra
(lah tee-**yay**-rah)

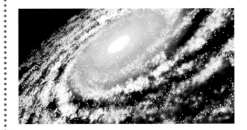

galaxy
la galaxia
(lah gah-**lahks**-ee-ah)

stars
las estrellas
(lahs es-**tray**-yahs)

Let's Talk
¡Hablamos!
(ah-**blah**-mos)

I want to be an astronaut.
Quiero ser astronauta.
(kee-**ay**-ro sayr ahs-tro-**now**-tah)

I want to be a pilot.
Quiero ser piloto.
(kee-**ay**-ro sayr pee-**lo**-toh)

skateboard
el monopatín
(el mo-no-pah-**teen**)

swing
el columpio
(el ko-**loom**-pee-o)

slide
el tobogán
(el toh-bo-**gahn**)

helmet
el casco
(el **kah**-sko)

to swing
columpiarse
(ko-loom-pee-**ahr**-say)

see-saw
el sube y baja
(el **soo**-bay ee **bah**-hah)

to jump rope
saltar a la cuerda
(sahl-**tahr** ah lah **kwayr**-dah)

in-line skates
los patines en línea
(los pah-**tee**-nays en **lee**-nee-ah)

roller skates
los patines
(los pah-**tee**-nays)

to play hide and seek
jugar a las escondidas
(hoo-**gahr** ah lahs
es-kown-**dee**-dahs)

bicycle
la bicicleta
(lah bee-see-**klay**-tah)

to skate
patinar
(pah-tee-**nahr**)

sandbox
el cajón de arena
(el kah-**hown** day
ah-**ray**-nah)

to ride a bike
montar en bicicleta
(mown-**tahr** ehn
bee-see-**klay**-tah)

Let's Talk

¡Hablamos!
(ah-**blah**-mos)

Do you want to play hide and seek?
¿Quieres jugar a las escondidas?
(kee-**ay**-rays hoo-**gahr** ah lahs
es-kown-**dee**-dahs)

Yes. Let's play.
Sí. Vamos a jugar.
(see **vah**-mos ah hoo-**gahr**)

team
el equipo
(el ay-**kee**-po)

baseball
el béisbol
(el **bays**-bowl)

coach
la entrenadora
(lah en-tray-nah-**dor**-ah)

soccer ball
la pelota de fútbol
(lah pay-**lo**-tah day **foot**-bowl)

to hit
pegar
(pay-**gahr**)

fan
el aficionado
(el ah-fee-see-o-**nah**-doh)

to score a goal
anotar un gol
(ah-no-**tahr** oon gol)

to catch
agarrar
(ah-gah-**rahr**)

baseball glove
el guante de béisbol
(el **gwahn**-tay day
bays-bowl)

football helmet
el casco de fútbol
(el **kahs**-ko day
foot-bowl)

baseball bat
el bate de béisbol
(el **bah**-tay day **bays**-bowl)

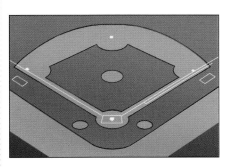

baseball diamond
el campo de béisbol
(el **kahm**-po day
bays-bowl)

football
el fútbol americano
(el **foot**-bowl ah-may-ree-
kah-no)

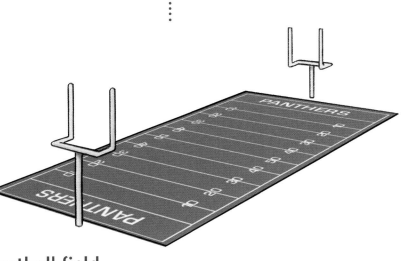

football field
el campo de fútbol
(el **kahm**-po day
foot-bowl)

to kick
patear
(pah-tay-**ahr**)

to tackle
taclear
(tah-klay-**ahr**)

to make a basket
marcar una canasta
(mahr-**kahr oo**-nah
kah-**nah**-stah)

basketball
el baloncesto
(el bah-lown-**says**-toh)

basketball net
la canasta
(lah kah-**nah**-stah)

to dribble
driblar
(**dree**-blahr)

to score a touchdown
marcar un touchdown
(mahr-**kahr** oon
tuch-down)

Let's Talk
¡Hablamos!
(ah-**blah**-mos)

We won the game!
¡Ganamos el partido!
(gah-**nah**-mos el pahr-**tee**-doh)

We played very well.
Jugamos muy bien.
(hoo-**gah**-mos **moo**-ee bee-**en**)

Winter fun

Las diversiones del invierno
(lahs dee-vayr-see-**on**-es day in-vee-**ayr**-no)

snow
la nieve
(lah nee-**ay**-vay)

to ski
esquiar
(es-kee-**ahr**)

skis
los esquís
(los es-**kees**)

snowboard
la tabla de esquiar
(lah **tah**-blah day
es-kee-**ahr**)

ice
el hielo
(el ee-**yay**-lo)

to skate
patinar
(pah-tee-**nahr**)

ice skates
los patines de hielo
(los pah-**tee**-nays day
ee-**yay**-lo)

to play hockey
jugar hockey
(hoo-**gahr hah**-kee)

hockey stick
el palo de hockey
(el **pah**-lo day **hah**-kee)

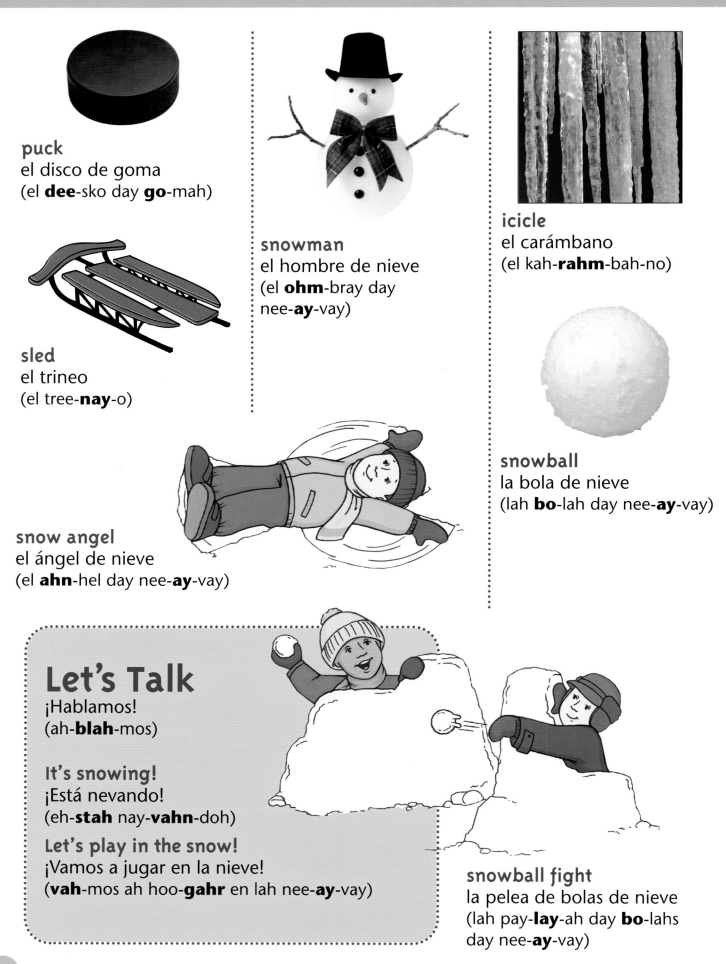

puck
el disco de goma
(el **dee**-sko day **go**-mah)

snowman
el hombre de nieve
(el **ohm**-bray day
nee-**ay**-vay)

icicle
el carámbano
(el kah-**rahm**-bah-no)

sled
el trineo
(el tree-**nay**-o)

snowball
la bola de nieve
(lah **bo**-lah day nee-**ay**-vay)

snow angel
el ángel de nieve
(el **ahn**-hel day nee-**ay**-vay)

Let's Talk
¡Hablamos!
(ah-**blah**-mos)

It's snowing!
¡Está nevando!
(eh-**stah** nay-**vahn**-doh)

Let's play in the snow!
¡Vamos a jugar en la nieve!
(**vah**-mos ah hoo-**gahr** en lah nee-**ay**-vay)

snowball fight
la pelea de bolas de nieve
(lah pay-**lay**-ah day **bo**-lahs
day nee-**ay**-vay)

train station
la estación de tren
(lah e-stah-see-**own**
day tren)

gas station
la gasolinera
(lah gah-so-lee-**nay**-rah)

police department
la comisaría de policía
(lah koh-mee-sah-**ree**-ah
day poh-lee-**see**-ah)

bank
el banco
(el **bahn**-ko)

barbershop
la peluquería
(lah pay-loo-kay-**ree**-ah)

fire department
la estación de bomberos
(lah e-stah-see-**own** day
bom-**bay**-ros)

supermarket
el supermercado
(el soo-payr-mayr-**kah**-doh)

Let's Talk
¡Hablamos!
(ah-**blah**-mos)

Where is the library?
¿Dónde está la biblioteca?
(**don**-day eh-**stah** lah bee-blee-o-**tay**-kah)

It is next to the bank.
Está al lado del banco.
(eh-**stah** ahl **lah**-doh del **bahn**-ko)

El **transporte**
(el trahn-**spor**-tay)

car
el coche
(el **ko**-chay)

ambulance
la ambulancia
(lah ahm-boo-**lahn**-
see-yah)

train
el tren
(el tren)

motorcycle
la motocicleta
(lah mo-toh-see-**klay**-tah)

bus
el autobús
(el ow-toh-**boos**)

airplane
el avión
(el ah-vee-**own**)

fire truck
el camión de bomberos
(el kah-mee-**own** day
bom-**bay**-ros)

Let's Talk
¡Hablamos!
(ah-**blah**-mos)

Are we going by train or by car?
¿Vamos en tren o en coche?
(**vah**-mos en tren o en **ko**-chay)

We're taking a plane!
¡Vamos en avión!
(**vah**-mos en ah-vee-**own**)

En el **campo** (en el **kahm**-po)

forest
el bosque
(el **bos**-kay)

lake
el lago
(el **lah**-go)

swamp
el pantano
(el pahn-**tah**-no)

mountain
la montaña
(lah mon-**tah**-nyah)

jungle
la jungla
(lah **hoong**-lah)

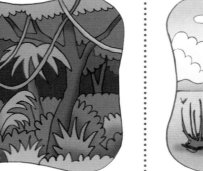

prairie
la pradera
(lah prah-**day**-rah)

island
la isla
(lah **ees**-lah)

Let's Talk
¡Hablamos!
(ah-**blah**-mos)

I want to go to the jungle.
Quiero ir a la jungla.
(kee-**ay**-ro eer ah lah **hoong**-lah)

Why? There are a lot of bugs there.
¿Por qué? Hay muchos insectos allá.
(por **kay** eye **moo**-chos een-**sayk**-tohs ah-**yah**)

To go **camping**
Ir de **campamento**
(eer day kahm-pah-**mayn**-toh)

tent
la tienda de
campaña
(lah tee-**yen**-dah day
kahm-**pah**-nyah)

campfire
la fogata
(lah fo-**gah**-tah)

flashlight
la linterna
(lah leen-**tayr**-nah)

map
el mapa
(el **mah**-pah)

compass
la brújula
(lah **broo**-hoo-lah)

sleeping bag
el saco de dormir
(el **sah**-ko day dor-**meer**)

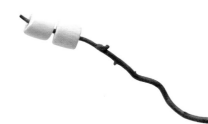

marshmallows
los malvaviscos
(los mahl-vah-**vee**-skos)

backpack
la mochila
(lah mo-**chee**-lah)

fishing pole
la caña de pescar
(lah **kah**-nyah day
pays-**kahr**)

grasshopper
el saltamontes
(el sahl-tah-**mon**-tays)

robin
el petirrojo
(el pay-tee-**ro**-ho)

to fish
pescar
(pays-**kahr**)

mosquito
el mosquito
(el mos-**kee**-toh)

ant
la hormiga
(lah or-**mee**-gah)

to hike
ir de caminata
(eer day kah-mee-**nah**-tah)

to go camping
ir de campamento
(eer day kahm-pah-**mayn**-toh)

Let's Talk

¡Hablamos!
(ah-**blah**-mos)

What is it?
¿Qué es?
(kay ays)

It's an owl.
Es un bujo.
(ays oon **boo**-ho)

horse
el caballo
(el kah-**by**-yo)

colt
el potro
(el **po**-tro)

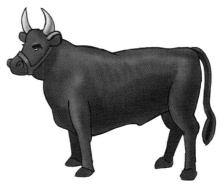

bull
el toro
(el **toh**-ro)

calf
el ternero
(el tayr-**nay**-ro)

sheep
la oveja
(lah o-**vay**-hah)

goose
el ganso
(el **gahn**-so)

cow
la vaca
(lah **vah**-kah)

lamb
el cordero
(el kor-**day**-ro)

duck
el pato
(el **pah**-toh)

pig
el cerdo
(el **sayr**-doh)

rooster
el gallo
(el **gah**-yo)

chick
el pollito
(el po-**yee**-toh)

piglet
el cochinillo
(el ko-chee-**nee**-yo)

hen
la gallina
(lah gah-**yee**-nah)

to hatch
salir del cascarón
(sah-**leer** del kah-
skah-**rown**)

Let's Talk
¡Hablamos!
(ah-**blah**-mos)

Look at the ducklings!
¡Mira los patitos!
(**mee**-rah los pah-**tee**-tohs)

They are so soft!
¡Qué suaves son!
(kay **swah**-vays sown)

lion
el león
(el lay-**own**)

hippopotamus
el hipopótamo
(el ee-po-**po**-tah-mo)

giraffe
la girafa
(lah hee-**rah**-fah)

tiger
el tigre
(el **tee**-gray)

lizard
el lagarto
(el lah-**gahr**-toh)

panther
la pantera
(lah pahn-**tay**-rah)

camel
el camello
(el kah-**may**-yo)

rhinoceros
el rinoceronte
(el ree-no-ser-**on**-tay)

ostrich
el avestruz
(el ah-vay-**stroos**)

monkey
el mono
(el **mo**-no)

bear
el oso
(el **o**-so)

panda
el oso panda
(el **o**-so **pahn**-dah)

gorilla
el gorila
(el go-**ree**-lah)

polar bear
el oso polar
(el **o**-so po-**lahr**)

kangaroo
el canguro
(el kahn-**goo**-ro)

Let's Talk
¡Hablamos!
(ah-**blah**-mos)

This elephant is really big!
¡Este elefante es muy grande!
(**es**-tay e-lay-**fahn**-tay ays **moo**-ee **grahn**-day)

Yes, and he weighs a lot.
Sí, y pesa mucho.
(see ee **pay**-sah **moo**-cho)

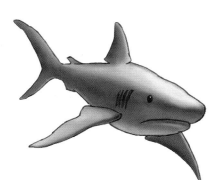

shark
el tiburón
(el tee-boo-**rown**)

seal
el foco
(el **fo**-ko)

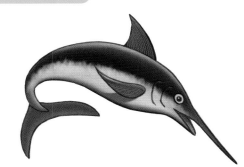

swordfish
el pez espada
(el pays ays-**pah**-dah)

whale
la ballena
(lah bah-**yay**-nah)

jellyfish
la medusa
(lah may-**doo**-sah)

seahorse
el caballito de mar
(el kah-bah-**yee**-toh
day mahr)

Let's Talk
¡Hablamos!
(ah-**blah**-mos)

Look! He's smiling.
¡Mira! Está sonriendo.
(**mee**-rah eh-**stah** sown-ree-**en**-doh)

I think he's hungry!
¡Creo que tiene hambre!
(**kray**-o kay tee-**en**-ay **ahm**-bray)

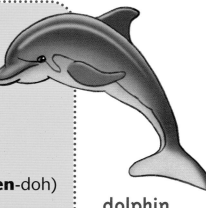

dolphin
el delfín
(el del-**feen**)

turtle
la tortuga
(lah tor-**too**-gah)

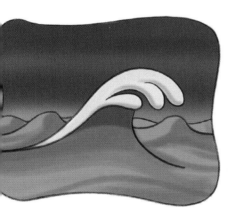

beach
la playa
(lah **ply**-yah)

beach ball
la pelota de playa
(lah pay-**lo**-tah day
ply-yah)

beach umbrella
la sombrilla
(lah som-**bree**-yah)

suntan lotion
la loción bronceadora
(lah lo-see-**own**
brohn-see-ah-**doh**-rah)

to swim
nadar
(nah-**dahr**)

waves
las olas
(lahs **o**-lahs)

to sunbathe
tomar el sol
(toh-**mahr** el sohl)

Let's Talk
¡Hablamos!
(ah-**blah**-mos)

Let's go swimming!
¡Vamos a nadar!
(**vah**-mos ah nah-**dahr**)

First, let's make a sand castle.
Primero, vamos a hacer un castillo de arena.
(pree-**may**-ro **vah**-mos ah ah-**sayr** oon kahs-**tee**-yo day ah-**ray**-nah)

movie
la película
(lah pay-**lee**-coo-lah)

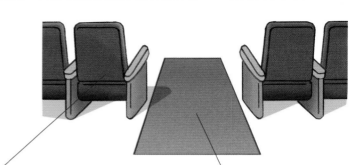

seats
los asientos
(los ah-see-en-**tohs**)

aisle
el pasillo
(el pah-**see**-yo)

ticket
el boleto
(el bo-**lay**-toh)

popcorn
las palomitas de maíz
(lahs pah-lo-**mee**-tahs day my-**ees**)

soda
el refresco
(el ray-**frays**-ko)

movie star
la estrella de cine
(lah es-**tray**-yah day
see-nay)

Let's Talk
¡Hablamos!
(ah-**blah**-mos)

Should we buy some popcorn?
¿Compramos unas palomitas de maíz?
(kom-**prah**-mos **oo**-nahs pah-lo-**mee**-tahs
day my-**ees**)

Yes, and I want a candy bar too.
Sí, y quiero un caramelo también.
(see ee kee-**ay**-ro oon kah-rah-**may**-lo
tahm-bee-**en**)

cotton candy
el caramelo americano
(el kah-rah-**may**-lo ah-may-ree-**kah**-no)

high wire
la cuerda de volatinero
(lah **kwer**-dah day vo-lah-teen-**ay**-ro)

ringmaster
el director de circo
(el dee-rek-**tor** day **seer**-ko)

trapeze artist
el artista del trapecio
(el ahr-**tees**-tah del trah-**pay**-see-o)

juggler
el malabarista
(el mah-lah-bah-**ree**-stah)

lion tamer
el domador de leones
(el doh-mah-**dor** day lay-**ow**-nays)

Let's Talk
¡Hablamos!
(ah-**blah**-mos)

I want to be a clown.
Quiero ser payaso.
(kee-**ay**-ro sayr peye-**ah**-so)

You're not very funny.
¡No eres muy divertido!
(no **ay**-rays **moo**-ee dee-vayr-**tee**-doh)

ballerina
la bailarina
(lah by-lah-**ree**-nah)

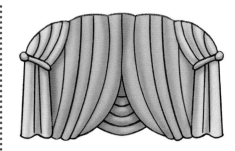

curtain
la cortina
(lah kor-**tee**-nah)

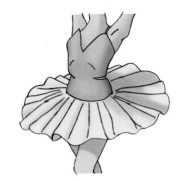

tutu
la faldita de ballet
(lah fahl-**dee**-tah day
bah-**lay**)

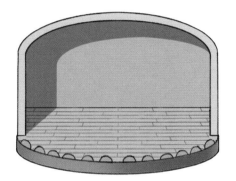

stage
el escenario
(el ay-say-**nah**-ree-o)

to applaud
aplaudir
(ah-plow-**deer**)

to bow
hacer una reverencia
(ah-**sayr oo**-nah ray-ver-
en-see-ah)

Let's Talk
¡Hablamos!
(ah-**blah**-mos)

Bravo!
¡Bravo!
(**brah**-vo)

I love the ballet!
¡Me encanta el ballet!
(may en-**kahn**-tah el bah-**lay**)

lights
las luces
(lahs **loo**-says)

En la **heladería**
(en lah ay-lah-der-**ee**-ah)

ice cream cone
el cono de helado
(el **ko**-no day ay-**lah**-doh)

vanilla
vainilla
(veye-**nee**-yah)

whip cream
crema batida
(**kray**-mah bah-**tee**-dah)

two scoops
dos copas
(dohs **ko**-pahs)

chocolate
chocolate
(cho-ko-**lah**-tay)

cup
el vaso
(el **vah**-so)

strawberry
fresa
(**fray**-sah)

Let's Talk
¡Hablamos!
(ah-**blah**-mos)

How much does a milkshake cost?
¿Cuánto cuesta una malteada?
(**kwahn**-toh **kwes**-tah **oo**-nah mahl-tay-**ah**-dah)

It costs three dollars.
Cuesta tres dólares.
(**kwes**-tah trays **doh**-lah-rays)

to marry
casarse
(kah-**sahr**-say)

bride
la novia
(lah **no**-vee-ah)

groom
el novio
(el **no**-vee-o)

veil
el velo
(el **vay**-lo)

bride's gown
el vestido de novia
(el ves-**tee**-doh day
no-vee-ah)

tuxedo
el traje del caballer
(el **trah**-hay del kah
bah-**yay**-ro)

Let's Talk
¡Hablamos!
(ah-**blah**-mos)

Look, he's going to kiss her!
¡Mira, la va a besar!
(**mee**-rah lah vah ah bay-**sahr**)

I don't like to kiss people!
¡No me gusta besar a la gente!
(no may **goo**-stah bay-**sahr** ah
lah **hayn**-tay)

wedding ring
el anillo de boda
(el ah-**nee**-yo day
bo-dah)

wedding bells
las campanas
(lahs kahm-**pah**-nahs)

wedding cake
el pastel de boda
(el pah-**stel** day **bo**-dah)

At the doctor's office

En la oficina del médico
(en lah o-fee-**cee**-nah del **may**-dee-ko)

doctor
el doctor
(el dohk-**tor**)

nurse
la enfermera
(lah en-fer-**may**-rah)

thermometer
el termómetro
(el ter-**mo**-may-tro)

bandage
la venda
(lah **ven**-dah)

broken arm
el brazo roto
(el **brah**-so **ro**-toh)

shot
la inyección
(lah een-yek-see-**own**)

fever
la fiebre
(lah fee-**ay**-bray)

Let's Talk
¡Hablamos!
(ah-**blah**-mos)

My throat hurts.
Me duele la garganta.
(may **dway**-lay lah gahr-**gahn**-tah)

You poor thing!
¡Pobrecita!
(po-bray-**see**-tah)

Community helpers

La gente de servicio público
(lah **hen**-tay day ser-**vee**-see-o **poo**-blee-ko)

police officer
la policía
(lah po-lee-**see**-ah)

garbage collector
el basurero
(el bah-soo-**ray**-ro)

librarian
la bibliotecaria
(lah beeb-lee-o-tay-**kah**-ree-ah)

postal carrier
el cartero
(el kahr-**tay**-ro)

bus driver
la conductor de autobús
(lah kon-dook-**tor** day au-toh-**boos**)

pharmacist
la farmaceuta
(lah fahr-mah-say-**oo**-tah)

Let's Talk
¡Hablamos!
(ah-**blah**-mos)

My father is a firefighter.
Mi padre es bombero.
(me **pah**-dray ays bom-**bay**-ro)

My mom is a police officer.
Mi mamá es policía.
(me mah-**mah** ays po-lee-**see**-ah)

traffic patrol
el policía de tránsito
(el po-lee-**see**-ah day **trahn**-see-toh)

Senses and feelings
Los sentidos y sentimientos
(los sen-**tee**-dohs ee sen-tee-mee-**en**-tohs)

to see
ver
(vayr)

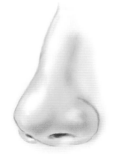

to hear
oír
(oy-**eer**)

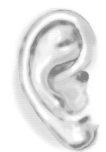

to smell
oler
(o-**layr**)

sad
triste
(tree-**stay**)

happy
contento
(kohn-**ten**-toh)

frustrated
frustrado
(froo-**strah**-doh)

angry
enojado
(en-o-**hah**-doh)

tired
cansado
(kahn-**sah**-doh)

proud
orgulloso
(or-goo-**yo**-so)

soft
suave
(**swah**-vay)

loud
fuerte
(foo-**ayr**-tay)

surprised
sorprendida
(sor-pren-**dee**-dah)

hard
duro
(**doo**-ro)

quiet
callado
(kah-**yah**-doh)

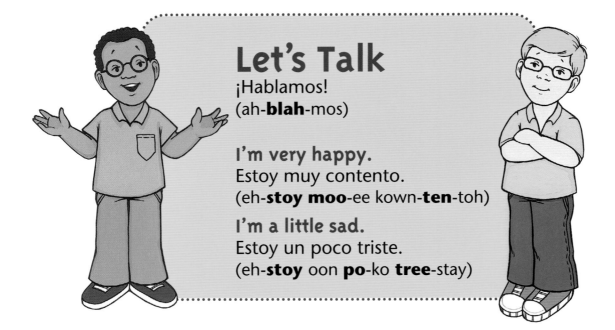

Let's Talk
¡Hablamos!
(ah-**blah**-mos)

I'm very happy.
Estoy muy contento.
(eh-**stoy moo**-ee kown-**ten**-toh)

I'm a little sad.
Estoy un poco triste.
(eh-**stoy** oon **po**-ko **tree**-stay)

Action words at home
Acciones en la casa
(ahk-see-**o**-nays en lah **kah**-sah)

to wake up
despertarse
(des-per-**tahr**-say)

to get dressed
vestirse
(ves-**teer**-say)

to drink
beber
(bay-**bayr**)

to wash your face
lavarse la cara
(lah-**vahr**-say lah **kah**-rah)

to eat
comer
(ko-**mayr**)

to watch TV
mirar la television
(mee-**rahr** lah tay-lay-vee-see-**own**)

to study
estudiar
(es-too-dee-**ahr**)

Let's Talk
¡Hablamos!
(ah-**blah**-mos)

Do you have any cavities?
¿Tienes caries?
(tee-**en**-ays kah-ree-**ays**)

No, I brush my teeth twice a day.
No, me lavo los dientes dos veces
al día.
(no may **lah**-vo los dee-**yen**-tays dohs
vay-says ahl **dee**-ah)

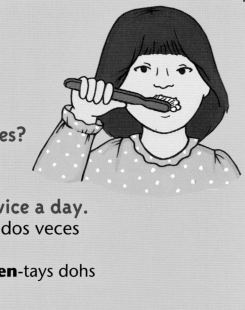

Action words for playing

Acciones del recreo
(ahk-see-**o**-nays del ray-**kray**-o)

to shout
gritar
(gree-**tahr**)

to chase
perseguir
(per-say-**geer**)

to climb
subirse
(soo-**beer**-say)

to whisper
susurrar
(soo-soo-**rahr**)

to run
correr
(ko-**rayr**)

to fall
caerse
(keye-**ayr**-say)

to jump
saltar
(sahl-**tahr**)

Let's Talk
¡Hablamos!
(ah-**blah**-mos)

Let's hide.
Vamos a escondernos.
(**vah**-mos ah es-kohn-**dayr**-nos)

Come on. Let's go to the basement.
Ven. Vamos al sótano.
(ven **vah**-mos ahl **so**-tahn-o)

Imagination words
Palabras de cuentos
(pah-**lah**-brahs day **kwayn**-tohs)

king
el rey
(el ray)

queen
la reina
(lah **ray**-nah)

prince
el príncipe
(el **preen**-see-pay)

princess
la princesa
(lah preen-**say**-sah)

fairy godmother
el hada
(el **ah**-dah)

knight
el caballero
(el kah-bah-**yay**-ro)

wand
la varita mágica
(lah vah-**ree**-tah **mah**-hee-kah)

dragon
el dragón
(el drah-**gohn**)

castle
el castillo
(el kah-**stee**-yo)

armor
la armadura
(lah ahr-mah-**doo**-rah)

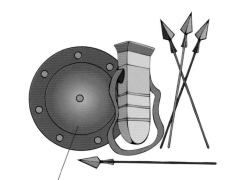

shield
el escudo
(el es-**koo**-doh)

unicorn
el unicornio
(el oo-nee-**kor**-nee-o)

sword
la espada
(lah es-**pah**-dah)

crown
la corona
(lah ko-**ro**-nah)

witch
la bruja
(lah **broo**-hah)

giant
el gigante
(el hee-**gahn**-tay)

monster
el monstruo
(el **mohn**-stroo-o)

ghost
el fantasma
(el fahn-**tahs**-mah)

pirate
el pirata
(el pee-**rah**-tah)

to fly
volar
(vo-**lahr**)

pirate ship
el barco de pirata
(el **bahr**-ko day
pee-**rah**-tah)

treasure
el tesoro
(el tay-**so**-ro)

Let's Talk
¡Hablamos!
(ah-**blah**-mos)

Once upon a time, there was a beautiful princess...
Había una vez una princesa
hermosa...
(ah-**bee**-ah **oo**-nah vays **oo**-nah
preen-**say**-sah er-**mo**-sah)

El **tiempo** (el tee-**aym**-po)

rainy
lluviosa
(yoo-vee-**o**-sah)

spring
la primavera
(lah pree-mah-**vay**-rah)

fall
el otoño
(el o-**toh**-nyo)

cloudy
nublado
(noo-**blah**-doh)

summer
el verano
(el vayr-**ahn**-no)

winter
el invierno
(el in-vee-**yayr**-no)

windy
ventoso
(ven-**toh**-so)

Let's Talk

¡Hablamos!
(ah-**blah**-mos)

What's the weather like?
¿Qué tiempo hace?
(kay tee-**aym**-po **ah**-say)

It's sunny.
Hace sol.
(**ah**-say sohl)

Days and months

Los días y los meses
(los dee-ahs ee los may-says)

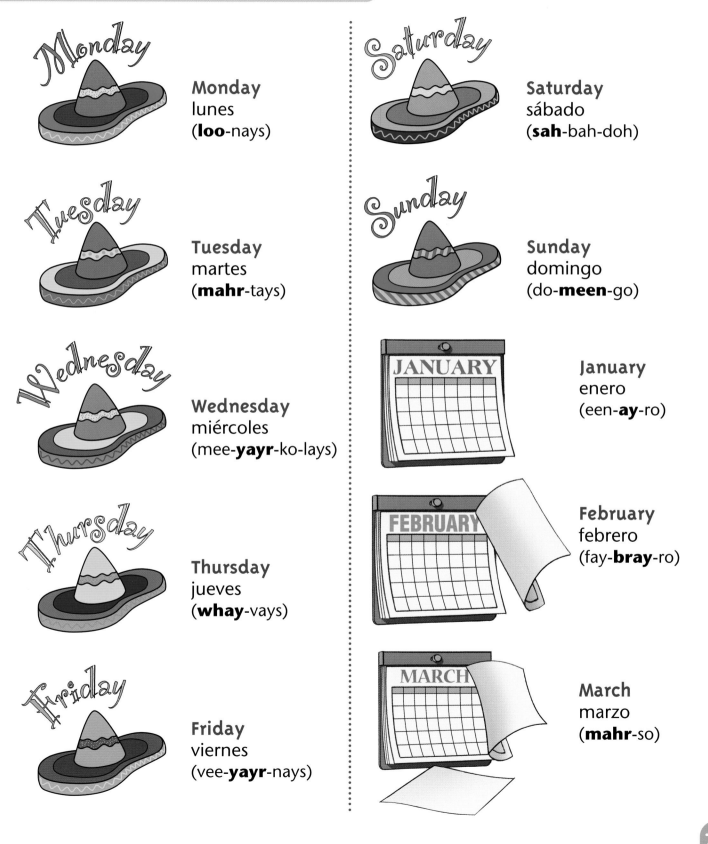

Monday
lunes
(**loo**-nays)

Tuesday
martes
(**mahr**-tays)

Wednesday
miércoles
(mee-**yayr**-ko-lays)

Thursday
jueves
(**whay**-vays)

Friday
viernes
(vee-**yayr**-nays)

Saturday
sábado
(**sah**-bah-doh)

Sunday
domingo
(do-**meen**-go)

January
enero
(een-**ay**-ro)

February
febrero
(fay-**bray**-ro)

March
marzo
(**mahr**-so)

73

April
abril
(ah-**breel**)

July
julio
(**hoo**-lee-o)

October
octubre
(ohk-**too**-bray)

May
mayo
(**my**-yo)

August
agosto
(ah-**go**-sto)

November
noviembre
(no-vee-**em**-bray)

June
junio
(**hoo**-nee-o)

September
septiembre
(sep-tee-**em**-bray)

December
diciembre
(dee-see-**em**-bray)

Opposites

Los opuestos (los o-poo-ay-stos)

day
el día
(el **dee**-ah)

night
la noche
(lah **no**-chay)

shut
cerrado
(say-**rah**-doh)

open
abierto
(ah-bee-**yayr**-toh)

wet
mojado
(mo-**hah**-doh)

dry
seco
(**say**-ko)

fast
rápido
(**rah**-pee-doh)

slow
lento
(**layn**-toh)

big
grande
(**grahn**-day)

small
pequeño
(pay-**kay**-nyo)

clean
limpio
(**leem**-pee-o)

dirty
sucio
(**soo**-see-o)

tall
alto
(**ahl**-toh)

light
ligero
(lee-**hay**-ro)

heavy
pesado
(pay-**sah**-doh)

short
bajo
(**bah**-ho)

Let's Talk
¡Hablamos!
(ah-**blah**-mos)

My turtle is very fast.
Mi tortuga es muy rápida.
(mee tor-**too**-gah ays **moo**-ee
rah-pee-da)

Are you kidding?
¿Estás bromeando?
(eh-**stahs** bro-mee-**ahn**-doh)

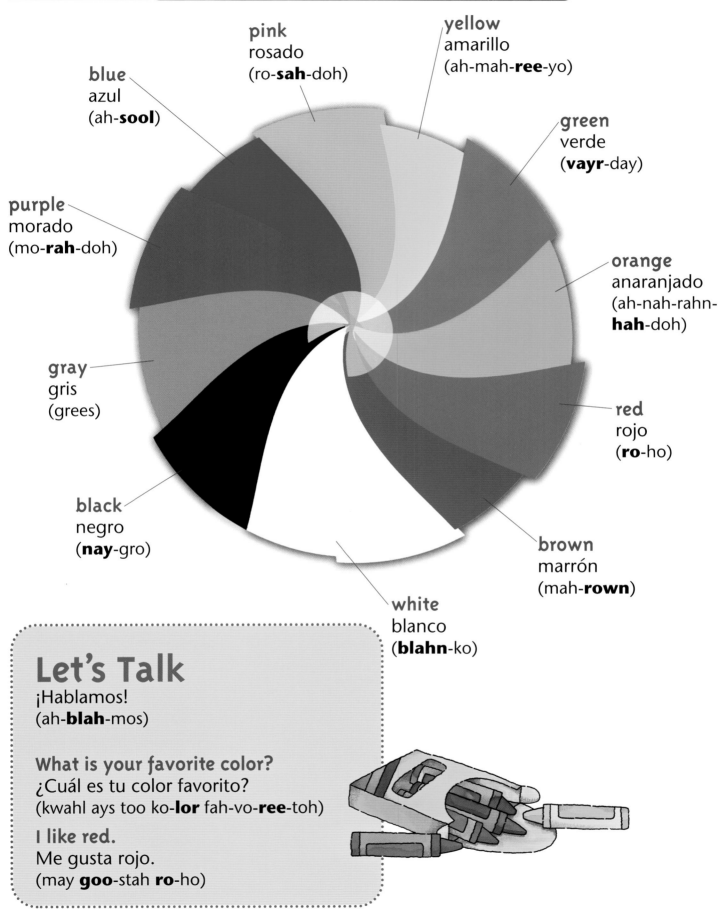

blue
azul
(ah-**sool**)

pink
rosado
(ro-**sah**-doh)

yellow
amarillo
(ah-mah-**ree**-yo)

green
verde
(**vayr**-day)

purple
morado
(mo-**rah**-doh)

orange
anaranjado
(ah-nah-rahn-**hah**-doh)

gray
gris
(grees)

red
rojo
(**ro**-ho)

black
negro
(**nay**-gro)

brown
marrón
(mah-**rown**)

white
blanco
(**blahn**-ko)

Let's Talk
¡Hablamos!
(ah-**blah**-mos)

What is your favorite color?
¿Cuál es tu color favorito?
(kwahl ays too ko-**lor** fah-vo-**ree**-toh)

I like red.
Me gusta rojo.
(may **goo**-stah **ro**-ho)

rectangle
el rectángulo
(el rec-**tahn**-goo-lo)

square
el cuadrado
(el kwah-**drah**-doh)

star
la estrella
(lah es-**tray**-yah)

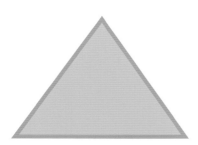

circle
el círculo
(el **seer**-koo-lo)

heart
el corazón
(el ko-rah-**sohn**)

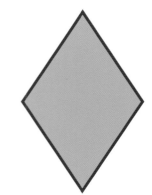

diamond
el diamante
(el dee-ah-**mahn**-tay)

triangle
el triángulo
(el tree-**ahn**-goo-lo)

Let's Talk
¡Hablamos!
(ah-**blah**-mos)

Do you know how to draw a heart?
¿Sabes dibujar un corazón?
(**sah**-bays dee-boo-**hahr** oon ko-rah-**sohn**)

Yes, and I can draw a diamond, too.
Sí, y también puedo dibujar un diamante.
(see ee tahm-bee-**en pway**-doh dee-boo-**hahr** oon dee-ah-**mahn**-tay)

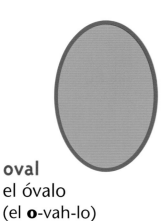

oval
el óvalo
(el **o**-vah-lo)

Numbers

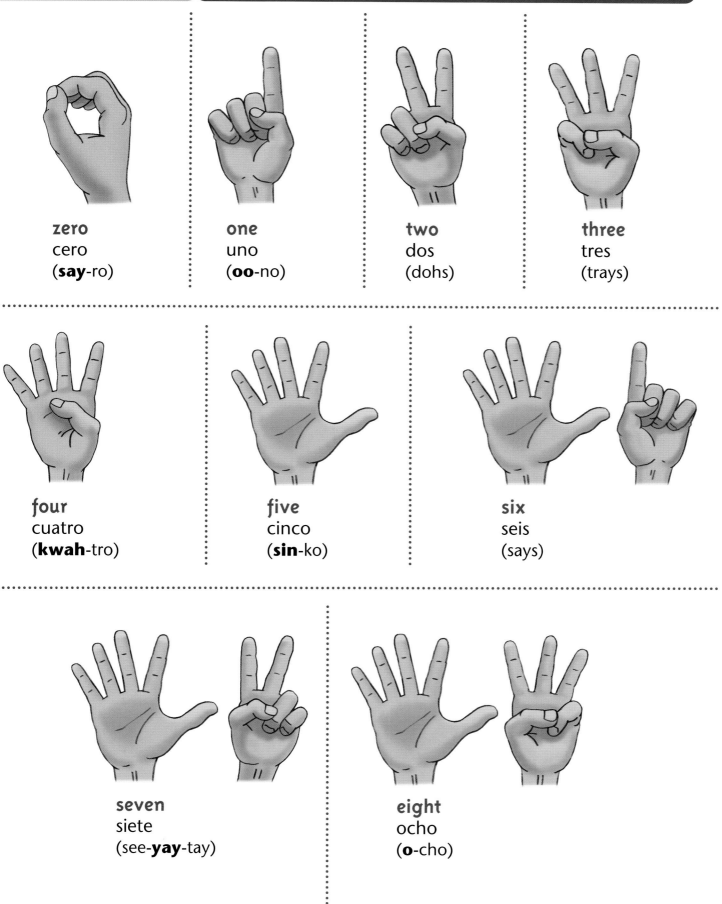

zero
cero
(**say**-ro)

one
uno
(**oo**-no)

two
dos
(dohs)

three
tres
(trays)

four
cuatro
(**kwah**-tro)

five
cinco
(**sin**-ko)

six
seis
(says)

seven
siete
(see-**yay**-tay)

eight
ocho
(**o**-cho)

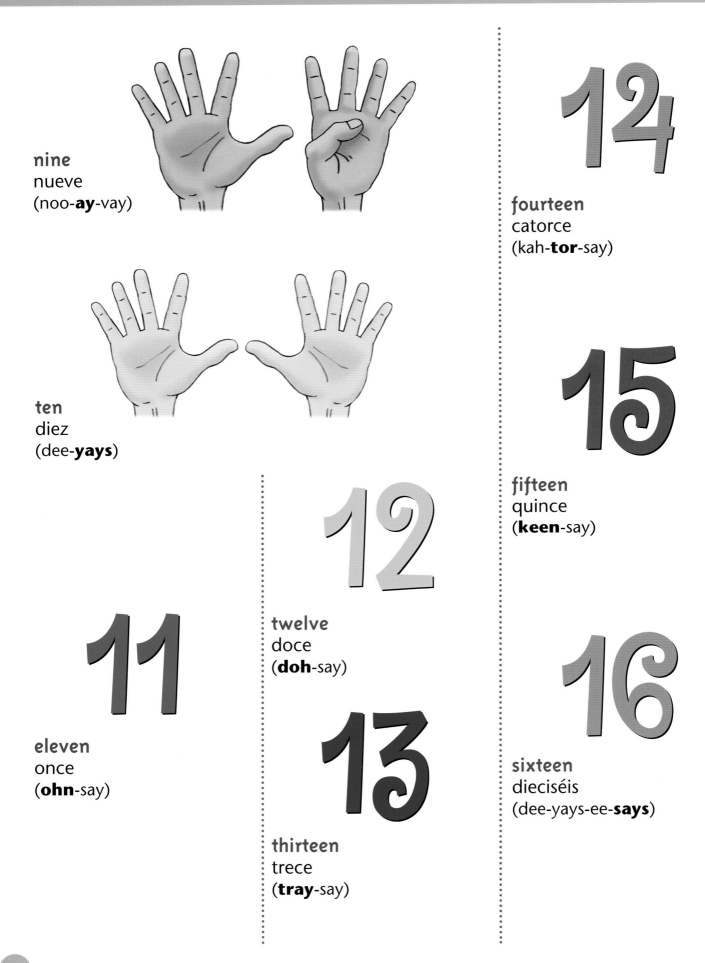

nine
nueve
(noo-**ay**-vay)

ten
diez
(dee-**yays**)

eleven
once
(**ohn**-say)

twelve
doce
(**doh**-say)

thirteen
trece
(**tray**-say)

fourteen
catorce
(kah-**tor**-say)

fifteen
quince
(**keen**-say)

sixteen
dieciséis
(dee-yays-ee-**says**)

seventeen
diecisiete
(dee-yays-ee-see-**yay**-tay)

eighteen
dieciocho
(dee-yays-ee-**o**-cho)

nineteen
diecinueve
(dee-yays-ee-noo-**ay**-vay)

20

twenty
veinte
(**vayn**-tay)

a hundred
un ciento
(oon see-**en**-toh)

a thousand
un mil
(oon meel)

1,000,000

a million
un million
(oon mee-**yohn**)

a billion
un billion
(oon bee-**yohn**)

Let's Talk
¡Hablamos!
(ah-**blah**-mos)

How old are you?
¿Cuántos años tienes?
(**kwahn**-tohs **ah**-nyos tee-**en**-ays)

I am six years old.
Tengo seis años.
(**tayn**-go says **ah**-nyos)

Location words
Palabras de posición
(pah-**lah**-brahs day po-see-see-**ohn**)

on
sobre
(**so**-bray)

in
en
(ayn)

between
entre
(**ayn**-tray)

under
debajo
(day-**bah**-ho)

behind
detrás
(day-**trahs**)

on top
encima
(ayn-**see**-mah)

far
lejos
(**lay**-hos)

near
cerca
(**sayr**-kah)

bottom
base
(**bah**-say)

top
parte de arriba
(**pahr**-tay day ah-**ree**-bah)

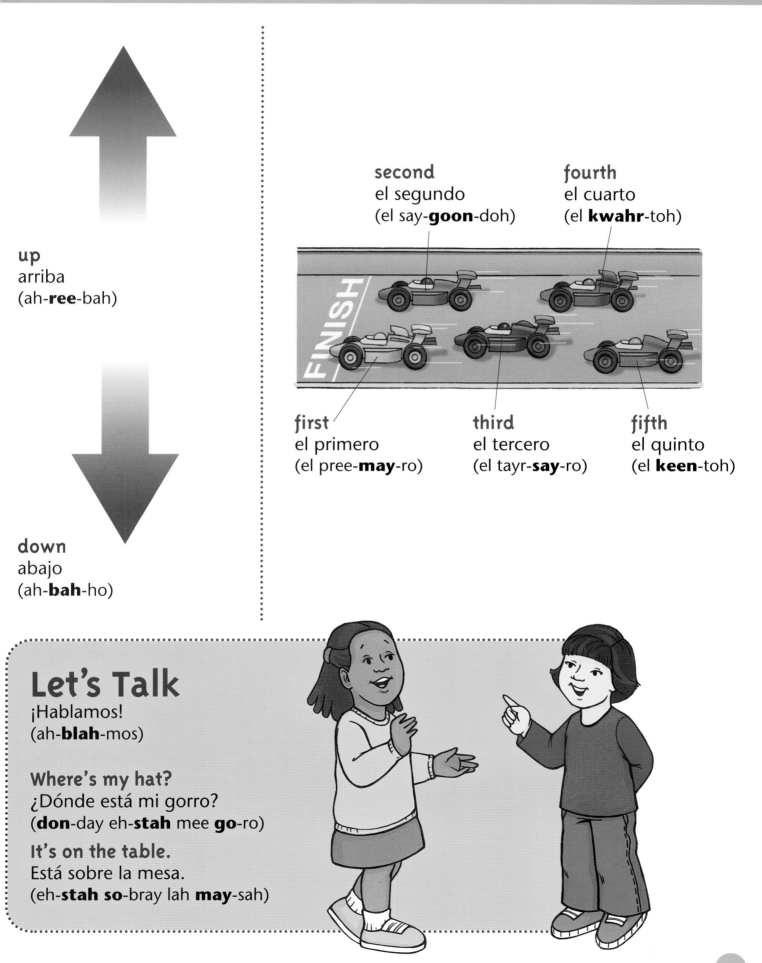

up
arriba
(ah-**ree**-bah)

down
abajo
(ah-**bah**-ho)

second
el segundo
(el say-**goon**-doh)

fourth
el cuarto
(el **kwahr**-toh)

first
el primero
(el pree-**may**-ro)

third
el tercero
(el tayr-**say**-ro)

fifth
el quinto
(el **keen**-toh)

FINISH

Let's Talk
¡Hablamos!
(ah-**blah**-mos)

Where's my hat?
¿Dónde está mi gorro?
(**don**-day eh-**stah** mee **go**-ro)

It's on the table.
Está sobre la mesa.
(eh-**stah so**-bray lah **may**-sah)

Good morning, Emy!
¡Buenos días, Emy!
(**bway**-nos **dee**-ahs **em**-mee)

Hi, Dad!
¡Hola, Papá!
(**o**-lah pah-**pah**)

I'm hungry.
Tengo hambre.
(**tayn**-go **ahm**-bray)

Me too. Let's eat breakfast.
Yo también. Vamos a tomar el desayuno.
(yo tahm-bee-**en vah**-mos ah toh-**mahr** el des-ah-**yoo**-no)

What day is today?
¿Qué día es hoy?
(kay **dee**-ah ays oy)

Today is Monday.
Hoy es lunes.
(oy ays **loo**-nays)

What time is it?
¿Qué hora es?
(kay **o**-rah ays)

It's eight o'clock.
Son las ocho.
(sohn lahs **o**-cho)

Goodbye, Mom! I love you.
¡Hasta luego, Mamá! Te quiero.
(**ah**-stah loo-**ay**-go mah-**mah** tay kee-**ay**-ro)

Bye, honey. Have a good day.
Adiós, mi vida. Que tengas un buen día.
(ah-dee-**os** mee **vee**-dah kay **tayn**-gahs oon bwayn **dee**-ah)

Do you know how to play basketball?
¿Sabes jugar baloncesto?
(**sah**-bays hoo-**gahr** bah-lown-**says**-toh)

Do you have any brothers and sisters?
¿Tienes hermanos?
(tee-**en**-ays er-**mah**-nos)

I have three sisters.
Tengo tres hermanas.
(**tayn**-go trays er-**mah**-nahs)

How old is Zack?
¿Cuántos años tiene Zack?
(**kwahn**-tohs **ah**-nyos tee-**en**-ay zak)

He is six years old.
Tiene seis años.
(tee-**en**-ay says **ah**-nyos)

Yes, I love sports.
Sí, me encantan mucho los deportes.
(see may ayn-**kahn**-tahn **moo**-cho los day-**por**-tays)

Emy, this is Josh. He is new.
Emy, te presento a Josh. Es nuevo.
(**em**-mee tay pray-**sayn**-toh ah josh ays noo-**ay**-vo)

Hi! Do you want to play with me?
¡Hola! ¿Quieres jugar conmigo?
(**o**-lah kee-**ay**-rays hoo-**gahr** kohn-**mee**-go)

See you later!
¡Hasta la vista!
(**ah**-stah lah **vee**-stah)

Bye, John!
¡Adiós, John!
(ah-dee-**ohs** jahn)

Do you want to play with Mark?
¿Quieres jugar con Mark?
(kee-**ay**-rays **hoo**-gahr kohn mahrk)

Can I watch TV?
¿Puedo mirar la televisión?
(**pway**-doh mee-**rahr** lah tay-lay-vee-see-**own**)

What do you want to do?
¿Qué quieres hacer?
(kay kee-**ay**-rays ah-**sayr**)

Let's go to the swings.
Vamos a los columpios.
(**vah**-mos ah los ko-**loom**-pee-os)

How was school today?
¿Cómo te fue en la escuela hoy?
(**ko**-mo tay fway en lah es-**kway**-lah oy)

I have a new friend.
Tengo un nuevo amigo.
(**tayn**-go oon noo-**ay**-vo ah-**mee**-go)

That's great, sweetheart. What's your friend's name?
¡Qué bien, cariño! ¿Cómo se llama tu amigo?
(kay bee-**en** kah-**ree**-nyo **ko**-mo say **yah**-mah too ah-**mee**-go)

His name is Joe.
Se llama Joe.
(say **yah**-mah jo)

Brush your teeth, Mary.
Lávate los dientes, Mary.
(**lah**-vah-tay los
dee-**yen**-tays **mayr**-ee)

I already did, Mom.
Ya lo hice, Mamá.
(yah lo **ee**-say mah-**mah**)

Give me a kiss.
Dame un beso.
(**dah**-may oon **bay**-so)

I love you very much, Mommy.
Te quiero mucho, Mamá.
(tay kee-**ay**-ro **moo**-cho mah-**mah**)

Good night, Josh! See you tomorrow!
¡Buenas noches, Josh! ¡Hasta mañana!
(**bway**-nahs **no**-chays josh **ah**-stah
mah-**nya**-nah)

Good night, Mommy!
¡Buenas noches, Mamá!
(**bway**-nahs **no**-chays mah-**mah**)

Index

English to Spanish

drum	. . . .	.el tambor, 37
dry	. . . .	.seco, 75
dryer	. . . .	.la secadora, 27
duck	. . . .	.el pato, 52
dustpan	. . . .	.el recogedor, 27
ear	. . . .	.la oreja, 9
earrings	. . . .	.los aretes, 16
earth	. . . .	.la tierra, 39
eat, to	. . . .	.comer, 67
egg	. . . .	.el huevo, 23
eight	. . . .	.ocho, 79
eighteen	. . . .	.dieciocho, 81
elbow	. . . .	.el codo, 11
eleven	. . . .	.once, 80
eraser	. . . .	.el borrador, 34
eye	. . . .	.el ojo, 9
eyebrows	. . . .	.las cejas, 10
eyelashes	. . . .	.las pestañas, 9
fairy godmother	. . . .	.el hada, 69
fall	. . . .	.el otoño, 72
fall, to	. . . .	.caerse, 68
fan	. . . .	.el aficionado, 42
far	. . . .	.lejos, 82
fast	. . . .	.rápido, 75
father	. . . .	.el padre, 7
favors	. . . .	.los recuerdos, 33
February	. . . .	.febrero, 73
fever	. . . .	.la fiebre, 63
fifteen	. . . .	.quince, 80
fifth	. . . .	.el quinto, 83
finger	. . . .	.el dedo, 11
fire department	. . . .	.la estación de bomberos, 47
fire truck	. . . .	.el camión de bomberos, 48
fireplace	. . . .	.el hogar, 19
first	. . . .	.el primero, 83
fish	. . . .	.el pescado, 24
fish, to	. . . .	.pescar, 51
fishing pole	. . . .	.la caña de pescar, 50
five	. . . .	.cinco, 79
flashlight	. . . .	.la linterna, 50
flowerpot	. . . .	.la maceta, 29
flute	. . . .	.la flauta, 37
fly, to	. . . .	.volar, 71
foot	. . . .	.el pie, 12
football	. . . .	.el fútbol americano, 43
football field	. . . .	.el campo de fútbol, 43
football helmet	. . . .	.el casco de fútbol, 43
forehead	. . . .	.el frente, 9
forest	. . . .	.el bosque, 49
fork	. . . .	.el tenedor, 26
four	. . . .	.cuatro, 79
fourteen	. . . .	.catorce, 80
fourth	. . . .	.el cuarto, 83
Friday	. . . .	.viernes, 73
frustrated	. . . .	.frustrado, 65
frying pan	. . . .	.el sartén, 22
galaxy	. . . .	.la galaxia, 39
garage	. . . .	.el garaje, 18
garbage collector	. . . .	.el basurero, 64
gas station	. . . .	.la gasolinera, 47
get dressed, to	. . . .	.vestirse, 67
ghost	. . . .	.el fantasma, 70
giant	. . . .	.el gigante, 70
giraffe	. . . .	.la girafa, 54
glass	. . . .	.el vaso, 26
glasses	. . . .	.los lentes, 10
gloves	. . . .	.los guantes, 14
glue	. . . .	.el pegamento, 35
gold	. . . .	.oro, 16
goose	. . . .	.el ganso, 52

gorilla	. . . .	.el gorila, 55
grandfather	. . . .	.el abuelo, 7
grandmother	. . . .	.la abuela, 7
grapes	. . . .	.las uvas, 25
grasshopper	. . . .	.el saltamontes, 51
gray	. . . .	.gris, 77
green	. . . .	.verde, 77
groom	. . . .	.el novio, 62
guinea pig	. . . .	.el cobaya, 28
guitar	. . . .	.la guitarra, 37
ham	. . . .	.el jamón, 24
hammer	. . . .	.el martillo, 30
hand	. . . .	.la mano, 11
happy	. . . .	.contento, 65
hard	. . . .	.duro, 66
harmonica	. . . .	.la harmónica, 37
hat	. . . .	.el gorro, 15
hatch, to	. . . .	.salir del cascarón, 53
hear, to	. . . .	.oír, 65
heart	. . . .	.el corazón, 78
heavy	. . . .	.pesado, 76
helmet	. . . .	.el casco, 40
hen	. . . .	.la gallina, 53
high wire	. . . .	.la cuerda de volatinero, 59
hike, to	. . . .	.ir de caminata, 51
hip	. . . .	.la cadera, 11
hippopotamus	. . . .	.el hipopótamo, 54
hit, to	. . . .	.pegar, 42
hockey stick	. . . .	.el palo de hockey, 45
homework	. . . .	.la tarea, 36
horse	. . . .	.el caballo, 52
house	. . . .	.la casa, 17
hug, to	. . . .	.abrazar, 8
hundred, a	. . . .	.un ciento, 81
ice	. . . .	.el hielo, 45
ice cream cone	. . . .	.el cono de helado, 61
ice skates	. . . .	.los patines de hielo, 45
icicle	. . . .	.el carámbano, 46
in	. . . .	.en, 82
in-line skates	. . . .	.los patines en línea, 40
iron	. . . .	.la plancha, 27
ironing board	. . . .	.el tabla de planchar, 27
island	. . . .	.la isla, 49
jacket	. . . .	.la chaqueta, 14
January	. . . .	.enero, 73
jeans	. . . .	.los vaqueros, 13
jellyfish	. . . .	.la medusa, 56
juggler	. . . .	.el malabarista, 59
juice	. . . .	.el jugo, 23
July	. . . .	.julio, 74
jump, to	. . . .	.saltar, 68
jump rope, to	. . . .	.saltar a la cuerda, 40
June	. . . .	.junio, 74
jungle	. . . .	.la jungla, 49
kangaroo	. . . .	.el canguro, 55
keyboard	. . . .	.la teclada, 38
kick, to	. . . .	.patear, 43
king	. . . .	.el rey, 69
kiss, to	. . . .	.besar, 8
kitchen	. . . .	.la cocina, 17
kittens	. . . .	.los gatitos, 28
knee	. . . .	.el rodillo, 12
knife	. . . .	.el cuchillo, 26
knight	. . . .	.el caballero, 69
ladybug	. . . .	.la mariquita, 29
lake	. . . .	.el lago, 49
lamb	. . . .	.el cordero, 52
lamp	. . . .	.la lámpara, 19
laptop	. . . .	.la computadora portátil, 38
laugh, to	. . . .	.reír, 8

second	.el segundo, 83
see, to	.ver, 65
seeds	.las semillas, 29
see–saw	.el sube y baja, 40
September	.septiembre, 74
seven	.siete, 79
seventeen	.diecisiete, 81
shampoo	.el champú, 21
shark	.el tiburón, 56
sheep	.la oveja, 52
shield	.el escudo, 70
shirt	.la camisa, 13
shoes	.los zapatos, 15
short	.bajo, 76
short hair	.pelo corto, 9
shorts	.los pantalones cortos, 13
shot	.la inyección, 63
shoulder	.el hombro, 11
shout, to	.gritar, 68
shut	.cerrado, 75
silver	.plata, 16
sing, to	.cantar, 33
sink	.el lavabo, 21, 22
sister	.la hermana, 7
six	.seis, 79
sixteen	.dieciséis, 80
skate, to	.patinar, 41, 45
skateboard	.el monopatín, 40
ski, to	.esquiar, 45
skirt	.la falda, 13
skis	.los esquís, 45
sled	.el trineo, 46
sleep, to	.dormir, 20
sleeping bag	.el saco de dormir, 50
slide	.el tobogán, 40
slow	.lento, 75
small	.pequeño, 75
smell, to	.oler, 65
sneakers	.los zapatos de lona, 15
snow	.la nieve, 45
snow angel	.el ángel de nieve, 46
snowball	.la bola de nieve, 46
snowball fight	.la pelea de bolas de nieve, 46
snowboard	.la tabla de esquiar, 45
snowman	.el hombre de nieve, 46
soap	.el jabón, 21
soccer ball	.la pelota de fútbol, 42
socks	.los calcetines, 14
soda	.el refresco, 58
soft	.suave, 66
soil	.la tierra, 29
soldiers	.los soldaditos, 31
spoon	.la cuchara, 26
spring	.la primavera, 72
square	.el cuadrado, 78
stage	.el escenario, 60
stairs	.las escaleras, 18
star	.la estrella, 78
stars	.las estrellas, 39
steak	.el bistéc, 24
stomach	.el estómago, 11
stove	.la estufa, 22
straight hair	.pelo lacio, 10
strawberry	.la fresa, 25, 61
students	.los alumnos, 34
study, to	.estudiar, 67
stuffed animal	.el animal de peluche, 31
summer	.el verano, 72
sun	.el sol, 39
sunbathe, to	.tomar el sol, 57

Sunday	.domingo, 73
suntan lotion	.la loción bronceadora, 57
supermarket	.el supermercado, 47
supper	.la cena, 26
surprised	.sorprendida, 66
swamp	.el pantano, 49
sweater	.el suéter, 13
swim, to	.nadar, 57
swing	.el columpio, 40
swing, to	.columpiarse, 40
sword	.la espada, 70
swordfish	.el pez espada, 56
tackle, to	.taclear, 44
take off, to	.quitarse, 15
tall	.alto, 76
teacher	.el maestro, 34
team	.el equipo, 42
teeth	.los dientes, 9
telephone	.el teléfono, 19
telescope	.el telescopio, 39
ten	.diez, 80
tent	.la tienda de campaña, 50
thermometer	.el termómetro, 63
third	.el tercero, 83
thirteen	.trece, 80
three	.tres, 79
Thursday	.jueves, 73
thousand, a	.un mil, 81
ticket	.el boleto, 58
tickle, to	.dar cosquillas, 8
tiger	.el tigre, 54
tired	.cansado, 65
toaster	.el tostador, 22
toe	.el dedo de pie, 12
toilet	.el inodoro, 21
tomato	.el tomate, 25
tongue	.la lengua, 9
toothbrush	.el cepillo de dientes, 21
toothpaste	.la pasta de dientes, 21
top	.parte de arriba, 82
towel	.la toalla, 21
toy cars	.los carritos, 31
traffic patrol	.el policía de tránsito, 64
train	.el tren, 32, 48
train station	.la estación de tren, 47
trapeze artist	.el artista del trapecio, 59
treasure	.el tesoro, 71
triangle	.el triángulo, 78
trumpet	.la trompeta, 37
T-shirt	.la camiseta, 13
Tuesday	.martes, 73
tulip	.el tulipán, 29
turn on, to	.encender, 38
turtle	.la tortuga, 28, 56
tutu	.la faldita de ballet, 60
tuxedo	.el traje del caballero, 62
twelve	.doce, 80
twenty	.veinte, 81
two	.dos, 79
two scoops	.dos copas, 61
type, to	.teclear, 38
uncle	.el tío, 7
under	.debajo, 82
underpants	.los pantalones interiores, 13
unicorn	.el unicornio, 70
up	.arriba, 83
vanilla	.vainilla, 61
veil	.el velo, 62
video game	.el juego de vídeo, 32
violin	.el violín, 37

Spanish to English